ALL BLACK
EVERYTHING

Kuhl House Poets

Mark Levine and Emily Wilson, series editors

ALL BLACK EVERYTHING

SHANE BOOK

UNIVERSITY OF IOWA PRESS   IOWA CITY

University of Iowa Press, Iowa City 52242

Copyright © 2023 by Shane Book

uipress.uiowa.edu

Printed in the United States of America

ISBN: 978-1-60938-923-9

ISBN: 978-1-60938-924-6

Text design and typesetting: Nicole Hayward. Dingbat graphic: iStock/OleksiiK.

Printed on acid-free paper

Cataloging-in-Publication data is on file with the Library of Congress.

Cover art: Jack Whitten, *Black Monolith V, Full Circle: For LeRoi Jones A.K.A. Amiri Baraka* (2014). Acrylic on canvas, 84 x 63 x 4 inches. © Jack Whitten Estate. Courtesy the Jack Whitten Estate and Hauser & Wirth. Private Collection, U.S.A. Photo by John Berens Photography.

For the Culture

"To Feel is perhaps the most terrifying thing in this society."
—CECIL TAYLOR

"I'll know when I find the ultimate sound."
—SONNY ROLLINS

Contents

ALL BLACK
EVERYTHING

Africa to Almost Spain: A Migration

1.

The storm blew me overboard.

It was there,
it led into my holes,
it was there beyond the barbed filament perimeter
I found my car—
blankets on the sunroof weighed down by tire irons,
rugs on windscreen held on by old tires,
interior surfaces roseflesh, edged
phosphorescent in evening greenfat,
winged crawlers massed along
the walls in twin clumps
like lung sacs.
They checked my hair.

2.

Book-less shelf,
pyramid altar of red, yellow
cans labeled "Café Bustelo," crafted

by ex-farmers
high in the verdant hills,
inner weathers.

One turned over, spread its leathered ass.

One with longest legs of day lazed on its tumescent boom box
throwing a soft pose. Tourniquet music.

One milked a breeze from a great cloudy thigh.

One jiggled its chest like a wheaty breakfast.

One jiggled its dew point.

3.

I walked out.
I walked for miles
and then I crawled.

The trees wended and wended
and then ended in me,
in rain-less sand.

And sand-less rain.
And rain-bending skies
reddening over another burly sea.

Everywhere I looked, bits of the next
ship I'd pre-paid to ride
set in the clay coastline

like sparse teeth
of fleshy
punched faces.

I waved myself into dusk,
zagging back as when a rocket
after-flares across night.

Back to my car
without a mic to tar.

4.

On a high note,
lapped seven and a half times
by one ever-gliding day,
a chalky music
in a quiet new bark.
Near the far shore, night scopes caught me,
marched me to razor perimeter,
blood-diamond days.

I worked up feeling.
I was not traffic.
I woke (cuffs) aboard a plane back to Africa.

5.

The sea is bigger than a purse.
The sea is a bag with a zipper,
a black skin suitcase.
The New World's opening begins
with the Old World tugging its bulging
custom-made shins and ashtrays,
flag of cross-legged human waving,
metal lamp tree,
rose-petal fan,
three blonde wood iron-legged chairs.

Country Music

I had a smell. It was hot inside. It was fixed between my eyes
and also blinking from the heavens: ticking eclipse
hedging it in light, like a morning moto-taxi ripping past
my window, descending his passengers into the sun.
I had to go to the city called Savior, the city called Beautiful
Horizon,
city called River of July. I feared for my smell.
The conmen, muggers, raised knives, diesel shouts.
In your curling intuition where the velocity of things
slimes along like a blue snail, you give me the map of my coming
swath, you here, helped only by glittering sidewalks,
you're so alone! And yet so generous, I thought, packing my cutlass
for my trip across the Bay of Paints. In my sack I packed a picture
of you
in your hair at the end of the dock, thinking no doubt of someone
else's
safety, considering the cities until beautiful sun collapsed behind
your head,
as I had done years before on a torchlit street.

The Map

Gusts pitted its red wall, intestinal
serpents no longer uncoiled.
It fell out like mud. Had moisture.
A center. And at its double-helix throat, hair-sheen.
Tried fieldwork but that weren't
for we. The swooshing volume.
The hot brick dances. The persistent initiates
at the mystery favela festival
feting mystery, sending concentric dust-palavers winging
back across the sea as wizened rooks.
Sorted the bitter leaves.
Snorted occasional threads.
We were Indoor Boy,
motorized by a rickety, lime-oil fuelled
flame in our calabash armor.
Amor, we said, please, we improve, we polish
the shells in shea butter and smoke-laden sap.
Our gourd machinist was under.
And the stream of inquiry chilled
our pivot-needle to a shudder.
Waters roared over the lip,
domes of mist smelling of horse sweat.
Would have defended with stereophonics
the wailing; the painted-on lust;
the candied yam allergens set aloft
and spinning; the great dropped rock.
Not now.
From behind brightly muraled,
corrugated tin, an irregular beating
fell out on the dirt street: round, large,

like a severed head.
Pulled on the vine and it buckled
the fine mesh.
The braided snakes. The irons.
The sudden wave. The hackles. The crime.

Modern

A light mist of beatings
settled all gorgeous
as most sunsets
tend to make us

feel better?—we could not feel
smaller, my executive.

It is custom.
It is feelings.
It is wolfed on fealty
to the meat marketing
board. And the meat.

Elsewhere: a furniture of emotion,
ambient sound
pleasantly hurtling us
toward the old waiting system.

My executive
continues to work for your executive.
The shed made of human skins
rings and rings

—to be re-cloaked
in our Dengue Fever Never Rains
off-island, if briefly
while everyone slept.

If my executive were reading
the smoke-stained stone architecture
my executive would know
the outbreak hordes

my executive drinks,
the bright day mossy,
the drippy light hurting our eyes,
forever-ed fever seeding fever among us,
and drinks, on a ferry ride.

Laos, Cambodia, Vietnam

From the visible world, we looked in
at soil broken by heat. Tents
mended in nomadic camp-shreds.
A farm of red birds
in everyone's sleep.
Swimming to a rock in the rapids
she climbed out and smashed the shell
of her wrist.
Foamy water hid the river's
calligraphy, the old sugar refinery's
corroded bars. Though earlier he sat listening,
his mouth now remembered nothing except
the bathroom.
I was tired enough of the weather and then you
reach behind my head and pull on a soft smoke rope
connected to those buffalo clouds.
The person beside me crosses herself.
The one from Miami motorcycles up the continent's
other side. We subtract ourselves
from the blistering heat spending the days at cathedrals
near the Pillory. Stabbings are as common
as thefts and everyone knows who does them.

S.T.A.R.S. (Strategic Tactical Armed Response Squad)

The forest clicked at me.
A lowered fence began
its creaking against the grass.
Mansions of corn, wind-flexed,
licked dudes sprawled
on the ground. Putative lemon de Ville
with the coupe leather seats,
cream soldiers, black berets
on big fro-ed heads. The force
is not something you
remember. It's the turtlenecks.
The dominating sugar
factory we lived in,
ready to light a river in two countries—
sorta enormous flotillas of checked
best Wycleffs, the brutal best friend,
a slap, a shot, slitting the pigs
and the thievery.
Pantherville,
let's see what settlements
we acquire. How many,
how many, how many,
how many. She know
she gotta
       keep me
some cash.
Until we're done
with all the thievery,
safeties off—

Next door homies gambling
on that game *Settlers of Wu Tang*.
Let's see what the settler does.

Kofi Mnemonic

There is a great sadness in this poorest of lands.
The only Lambo in the land belongs
to my Christian friend.
A Lambo is a Lamborghini,
a piece of Italian art
on blaster wheels.
Nightly, a piece of an Italian
is wheeled into the
lamb I'm always on the verge of—
the most precise steel in the most aggressive heels
of Italian steel ever felt in the sternum,
a chemical kind of power,
a space coupe dressed as
beauty
    shard
          flower.
Very hardcore business, man.
I'm a business, man.
Our dearest anthropologist always warns us
of past things: a blade song, a greed radio,
but y'all too busy tryna find
that blue-eyed hole. Me,
I let my black hair grow
and my stroke go
and my smoke mow
down my sweat
too much on the regular.
"We gonna glow-up the sky,
        give the whole 'hood a light show."

If it ain't
Fallujah hallelujah level
then I don't want
no more snow. I'm betting
on flip-flops, loose robes,
an RPG glow.
I'm like, goddamn,
I am not a Bleach Boy,
goddamn. When my boy's Lambo needs
repairs on the regular, he drives
the car up a ramp and onto a plane.
The monster's exhaust rockets
louder than a Carthaginian
elephant army rain.
He flies that beast business class
from Africa to Spain,
filled with hollow mangoes filled with
I-can't-feel-my-face things.
He collects the wildly metallic
patient that now scream-sings
in perfect punches
in his bankrupt country.
The roads are too wrecked
to wreck a piece of art blaster.
In a fortified garage, the car hulks.

Smallpox in Ibiza

I'm singing through
the auto-tune.

I'm crying through
the auto-tune.

The auto-tune is strong.
My eating game is long.

When the Canada Goose
jacket got the job

over me, I knew
we were in a new-old era,

the tallest
poured concrete column

in the world poured
out of a water hole

in the Caucasian sky.
Do you just believe in

nothing or do you grab
the gun and pray,

was the final menu
item that caught my eye.

I'm axing it
a strong question.

I'm waiting
for the start of Big Gulp

Season. I am
a strong question.

What Is the Matter

They sold me a trap

history they could dine to.

I took it. As one does. As you do.

As one would a tectonic

folk spritz paired

with a good schvitz

on my grind.

That was my mistake.

I have my heavily-seeded hairnets;

they have their massive armaments,

vote-rigged push force pool

bullies. It was not a fair fight, exactly.

We're not on the side

of constant rent, entirely,

and they say they want only

the young mullah

baby. A founder divine from

such twisted switches in

glitches and drone snitches

released from a hell-fire remix

prefigured in icing a homie.

Just outside the guilt

edged frame, photo-knifed in

two by the times and the drank.

That's they man.

Sarasota Sweats

The brother man

of another man

gravitated downwind

of a stereo

beeping, signatories

ululating at the

ceremonial signing

giving chips and dips,

daps and medal

blips to ex-flips—

all, totally signaling.

That's how they do.

They're giving us

a grey theory.

That's why we can't

wear the same blue-ish

force protector

singlet every damned

day into mysterioso

neighborhoods

of abuela-plated

good heat pouring

out of a magma

level smear.

That'd be cray.

And cray don't

cut it no more.

Juice Juice

All this talk about

who did what

to whom stays fresh

in these rooms with their

special skies, meeting

yourself again and again

coming faster

than water. No one talks

about Africa though

everyone has been—

its gift to us flying

of its own accord, not

frighteningly, just eating bugs.

To think is the hard thing:

we had a lake once

and now it's an ocean;

different altitudes,

sprays, ways of doing

things. It asks the questions

these days, with so many

interchangeable parts:

a fortress can be built

to a bay, a bay dug

up as a fleet of canoes,

planes, even a rubber

tree can curve

like a summer.

Going Forward

At last the Barbudos wear suits,
selling, selling into the deep

rhythms of the screen
cycling its venomous light rail

up and up, reverse waterfall
nano fork circuitous areole grease slit,

frost on the pain.
In the instep is shooting volts.

In the walking is wisdom.
Who this man

will not stop writing?
Him is have job.

Everything amped up
is unreal-real everything.

"Grenades detonate
when I enter the building."

It takes a muscle
to fall in love.

Caribbean Flex

Make I come check you, my baby.
Where I from, them who drink Lean
is mostly grown men
who eat they barbecue, drive
around in they slabs,
go home and make
love into brightly-colored stuffed animals.
I had a friend, once.
I put roses on the Panamera.
I put handclaps on the Guantanamera.
It all happened on an Instagram story whatever
hashtag DracoWeather; hashtag ThisAndThat.
Started at the bottom
and kissed on it.
Loved that bottom so much
I wanted to piss on it
(I never told you that).
Bless-up! Big-up!
These fully white-peopled cities
love recordings of dead Black people crooning
through hidden ceiling speakers above
the lettuce aisle
but don't want boujee Blacks
in the glass condo next door.
I get so lonely.
My friends are Ben and Jerry's
chunky Monkey.
I'm a chunky Negro Monkey.
We're natural friends.
The empty streets are emptied

at precisely eight o'clock. Gimme
another tub Saturday night alone
watching all my Black people on Netflix
give me death!
Same ting!
Lemme put on my Black Power beret
and scream slogans into an empty
Congo Peas can. I'll drown the words out
with the engine sound of the bathroom fan.
Lemme watch so much online porn I hurt
the fleshy-ribbed crook of my hand.
Lemme blast soca tracks way past
the rental condo 10 PM bylaw silence.
I lick my wrist. All night long
the shuttered grocery
store outdoor speaker gusts
the empty sidewalk with Grime:
Bae from India, hills of biryani,
meds so good, now I speak Gujarati.
I don't care.
I leave myself on read.
A corporation sprayed the condo walls
wet color before I got here.
And my dog, he's on probation
another five years. Skrrt-skrrt-skrrt.
I no go rush you, my baby.
From my balcony, I spied that gyal,
outrageous ting, but she can't see
'cause I got shades and ting. Now
I like collars, I like almonds

I'm not frontin', I like shining,
I'm blunted, I'm grinding
the dankest loud
into small, chiming twists
of melty space-time
that's for me to never know
and me to plead out.
Goddess of the goddam Sea!
Goddess of the goddam Sea!
Come forth, Buttah Cyat!

I Know I've Reached Peak Shane

You try living in a pigeon pen above a
series of car repair shops
and love motels for a while—
then come talk to me.
Real talk: this run-by-Queen-Victoria
British Empire outpost
of the history of the goddamn
complete world
—opium, Scottish
Presbyterian gangster shit,
the main flavor
profile for toothpaste, incidentally.
What a charge. Hit the past so hard
make it float-wait. I'm not
no Airbnb sucka,
I went to driving school,
drove a plug-in hybrid
sports car by Porsche
in my mind, 918 Spyder
maximum torque insect in my mind,
fastest electric coffin ever maimed.
All my niggas blew up like a brain drain
except me.
The cockpit is above
the mounds of fabric, ruffling
my waxen face.
I have a great LeBron face
for you.
And you, and you, and you.

All the Feels

Already knew what they wanted.
The earth liberation orchestra
never lies. Just look at the facts:
Carne Asada Shakur steady dropping
tracks from her cloud caster,
motorized Ottoman fashioned
of organic omega-threes,
thick caged West African prints wax-stamped
à la Shenzhen—and y'all wondering where
somebody hid? That the script notes only
point up the prude salad bar trifecta
cat cohorts short-selling on the strip,
none could be all that surprised.
Don't matter. Few notions stay
un-gentrified. Late night diner Mofongo
Afro Puff cereal *con* deep coat of mood
even laid down steep into blonder wood bowls
just won't quit
the Hot Beignets scent
from poured out Benjamins

like two small river berries touching

hairs into a beige-ness beyond

all convex metallic cones

grits exhalations of boots.

Dad Bod

I want to be happy

fuck you. Low rider magazine

easy-load for the AK

in a Black Liberation

Army birthday

type o' way. First thing

Imma do is grow

my movement beard,

feel some type o' way.

But you must live

in the Midwest,

be so inside

these landscaped

brethren

like a new gold scarf

underwater.

Why they making me

read this when I got no vote?

Pernicious malarian citizen

rocking the argue mandible,

it heard us. Say we're

the sunny side strangler

so what. This was

the new language.

Tippin' the Rafla on Three Wheels

Nah, before all that.
Sunrise. Just us dropping
on shocks, a pounce-spirit
muscling its way along

the street, mashed sounds
smashed to a shell-burnt
sulfur and all the oil neck
charms anyone could use.

Crucifix rope gold Virgin
de Guadalupe under
deepest midnight blue sky
beach towel lit by stars,

she pilots a crocodile across
the quarters, hood quieting
the dawn's sizzurp gleam.
Out beyond, amongst

the snarelight, nothing
but the guap promise,
a confessed relentlessness
depicted in the book of blizzards.

Real Sisters

I thumbed the single singed hair on my simple bell. They
maintained a latch key kid for me. We remained a slack-eyed id
for three. If the blanket was a thrown penumbra, the fire could
not have been more meaty. They are fairly hairless—hence their
aversion to snow. Who says the sun does not ride like a crouton
on the inner wires of a souped-up baby grand Camaro? Water
spots and parking heaters are often off a little mile. *Hey it's blowing
outside*, he would stammer into the phone, *just wanted to see what
you thought about that.* I've got motherboard approval to abduct my
theory. I've got the Lord's removal to instruct the symphony in A
minor misery. It is night and like the others I boil my weapons. A
wonderful gleam, or an eerie sickening thickness of the inner ear.

Mexico City Stole My Wife

Lingonberries the last diet hope,

she-blogger knitting together

a freedom, marauded through

by the state farmers and the blue

cornet l'amour. Turns out

fingers up to the Beyoncé birthers.

On deck: twin Jay-Z Jesuses.

Balsamic for thy word salada

you sail it slowly into the kale

meter, cranked by the gallant

Starboy shirts, previously

undid to the professed goodness

unsaid up in this stitch. One wanted

to make ear mirrors and sell

them in the Zócolo, drag off

all lyrical and shit. A portion

of mercy becomes a flora. A

flood perspective.

It's all about the honey. Little

perceptive resonance out of

prismic minutiae in

the graduate library of sounds.

We Have before Us

Wanna trade sheep
for roads?

People remind
you she had a name

dabbing, dabbing on them
like the usual.

Mystic with the stick do
juju. People dog you

bad and boujee,
maybe—but when's her novel

on the Afrofantastic
coming out?

Certain insect sounds,
the disembodied

alarm chimes,
bleed like a tat.

I dig it,
I eat clotted cream

with my pickles.
Suck like eight mink

they call me Octagon.
But when can we celebrate

another murder event
national vacation?

Slip them back in
like refillables.

They say crack kills.
Baby my crack sells.

I'm killing them.
Sorry for your loss, I got

Puma Suedes on my feet,
Mother I am stupid.

Girl, I think you gave
me cancer. Girl,

cocaine white
like boiled cassava,

I think you
just gave me

cancer. I dig it.
I eat rain. American

life coached me.
Join the Drip Club

make it rain.
Aim to live

in a jacuzzi.

Glock Weather

It's Glock weather. That's why
all my sweatpants are leather.
A set of older white people spies
me strolling the shuttered
downtown core. Away
with those purses,
pursed, lip-less lips.
They cross over.
It does not hurt a little,
human cross-over dribble
whatever.
I'm flossing, I'm sipping, steady tripping
pure Evian, no tap water,
I'm wearing fake Chinese fox fur
in these young money temps.
I own these times. No cap.
I been on the craziest wave, making nice
and now they wanna make me see ID.
Nice for what. That's the London
where they floss a lot.
You say you no go leave oh!
If you no sleep, I no go sleep.
Money long, my car too fast,
Aventador cherry body chocolate like a kitty cat.
Chilling in my inner Dubai, I get by.
My fire is fire.
My inside desert is lit. By the oil fires

of a thousand American bloodsuns,
they gon' make me interview again for it.

Next time I see him, waiting on line
at the fish bar, my Cape Verdean barber
tells me I been looking fly.
International flex. This the real face.
Après getting my hair did
at the only Black barbershop
in a slate-walled English town,
I feel this sound from the other side.
Who be that.

Ideology, or The Dream of the Guap-ified Field

Shorty see that drop, ask what I paid
I say, yeah I paid a guap.
Then I hit that switch that take
away the top. I change a money shower
into a thunder storm. Now I have to put
the whip's roof back up.
Guap is not $1000 or the exact amount of cash
down to the cent
needed to buy a fully-loaded-no-dents
Bentley. Guap is
strapping the pistol to my side,
got the oxygen mask, a favorite flask
of dirty fingers, I'm still preferring the ones
who don't get kidnapped. You run out
all Wordsworth on a trigger
while I'm steady stacking these racks,
I don't take naps,
I worked OT this week to get this guap,
a lot of money (a "pretty penny"
Guapo/Guapa
in a pretty shitty penny Spanish accent)—
as in big dad cows in Alberta, Texas,
got them guap horns I do not mess
with. My channel name
is Guap.
I don't know what you think
you got going on—
hanging from my pocket is a yacht
hanging from my neck is a plot.
Near lovely as Alexis, Texas,

the sun sets so low on the streets here
you could call it "hubcap."
Yo-James-Let's-Hit-The-Club,
let's lit the club right off the block,
I got mad guap to blow,
most often cash money,
showing high degrees of
purchase tower swagger
for fast-depreciation consumer honey:
luxury cars, electronics, power
to the people power.
All this to say, I beat
you fair and square in that race.
Anywhere you look,
you being watched hard
in the eye
of a money storm.

The Best Pozole in Santa Cruz

That big other
was like my big other
from another.

Was all,
"Imma kidnap your id,
make it feel like a litigant"

made it easy to work over
the No Knock Police Raid

(with the faulty funnel
for hazing trainees
stashed in the back room).

Bear. Hugged. Me.

Above the tiny trees
in the clamp-on forest, it ran
a biplane sky-banner reading:

GET THAT NEW RUG BABY, WE MAY BE HERE A WHILE...

That big other cold.
Its ringtone, the old hit:
Bubba Kush couch, you the one I lean on.

It was like it.

That big other needed
to get
born again—

Eat, Pray, Beyoncé,
or something

kept sending me out
to clean the display,
or something—

Das Kapital

While I try to fast-break blockchains
like Rest In Peace Harriet Tubman,
homies be broke from popping
bottle service bubbly. My way around it:
I ghost ride the Phantom with the loudspeaker
auto-tuning horror movie shout-laughs.
I'm so good, God,
satchels stuffed with green
made I live like an ambassador. God,
you good? Leaving pics on the Gram
then acting like you ain't know me is a lot
like The Dream of the Unified Sativa Field Theory
—any artist that can make a person
listen without fury
is next level. You sure you good? God,
I would come to where you at
but I'm dabbing wax with a shovel
going up the ladder.
They mad, make them madder.
They can't keep the pills
away from the profit.
Across my inner soul brother sprawls
a long money stain—no more slaving!
I ride with heat so, so, so
soo-woop in y'all's mofo clouds.
Gang-gang I make it rain.

Nice for What

I mean here. Is where.
The fuck. We should
always ever start.
Today, as we say to Wall Street
and the billionaire class,
Yo dawg, come thru
wit dat Fruit Roll-Up,
I still don't like maps,
me and the night sky are way too attached.
Right across the street from where we are
at this moment
is the City's largest power plant.
Yesterday I trimmed Bush Monster.
For all you know
I'm the United States Congress now.
That's the shit I'm talking 'bout though,
like you Prada-Man-I'm-Soda-Mouth
1000 Hemi-powered horses
direct from a factory,
the giant mushroom cap tendrilled
to everyone's head.
Be it resolved that it is
becoming a problem and let us be clear,
it is no secret that this
plant is located right next to the City's
largest public housing development,
nonetheless it was there
I learned Courvoisier and frenemies
is a Chex Mix type of mixture—you're shitting
me—and the largest campaign rally

of primary season sprung up
on Saturday. In support of environmental
racism, the powers that be are unhappy
you're here, throwing everything
to get people repeating.
I know you like to stay low.
I've been tweeting
what you leave under the maple.
Like a cam commandeering
a tortilla farmer
you cheesed me like a chatty man
which explains why Queen Street is poppin'
on Tuesdays. Dun kno!
Yeah Gucci, Ozwald Boateng and Kiton,
style tighter than a squeezing python,
the one and only
Prosecco popper, the cheddar doctor,
Achebe's words call me when they lonely,
I finesse down Boundary Road.
On their fashion-less asses
I been teaching classes
vaping wizard cabbage
welcome to the Sauce God Circle.
I wonder who's in this penthouse
tonight?! Airbus 380, man,
this thing's got spiral staircase, man!
I just hit a switch. Switch! Switch!
How I score them points.
This the spirit in the ghost site
right now, Scarborough ting from time, style,

sucker-free shades tabled
later on a power motion.
That's too old.
Times were hard in Puerto Rico.
We were dying, we are an island
surrounded by water, lots and lots
of water, ocean water.
That is a quote, this the flow.
Top left, those '97s look greezy fam,
we need to talk the "stealth exotic car" approach.
I don't know 'bout you
but now that Walcott's dead,
I feel I can write:
Oh you swaggy, huh?!
I started feelin' the burn when he came down,
no cameras, just him in a wheelchair
in a maniacal half-smile.
This is why I been sayin' "no new friends."
I'm so hot.
I'm so right now.
The time is now
to be uncompromising.
You know how this shit go, paying
no mind to the chicken heads lighting
fake friend fires
all up in my face.
I don't wanna tat
my name on anyone right now
so I know it's real.
The health of forty million people

lives in poverty, let's all get a field
away from the screens,
yo nice me
a juice box dawg.
I just need a reason
not to go out every evening.
These, I stan.
She was so arms,
she said I looked fat in my Caribana outfit
when the only heart attack
we should be talking about
is the one Wall Street is going to have.
Hair did, clothes dripped,
it's too late for all that Brother Love shit,
that "I'm your homie" tip,
waste yutes always mallratting smack my head,
wherein potential totes lies.
Make you dance to this.
Make you.
Let there be interviews like confessions,
twitter fingers turn to chicken fingers,
and you getting bodied by a bee's stinger?!
Your boy says he's the light-skinned Keith Sweat.
Well, I'm the light-skinned Boba Fett.
I'm not upset.
Putting prices on my head
is just impersonal
disrespectful disrespect.
That's social death
while September 20th

is just one of those days
when your life change
in other words,
I got more chune for your ear holes
so peep how you creep on my game,
watch Da Breakdown
but wake up and nothing's wrong,
'cept Penny finna get merked
if she tries to talk to my mans again.
Fear not. Two tokes
and I'm already blem fam—dirt long distance—
I need you—Patrice Lumumba—you
actin' kinda suspect,
keep callin' me Young X—
why the sudden genuflect?
Fake diamond earrings
till I return to the wrestling ring.
To be sure, there's no unreal rest here,
that's just your deflection.
The time is now to be vocal fried.
I no like wahala!
When I returned from it,
svelte and swaddled in a dark blue
pinstripe suit, I came to your door
and wept, right where slavery evolved
into Jim Crow
into Mass Incarceration
into The Realities We Have Today,
maybe to some he's *Tio*
maybe he's something else to you:

"Liquid" means rewind,
"the Gun Shot" means forward—
you requested it
so we rewind!
That's the flow.
Yo lowkey, Comfort Zone is lit style
you're so extra, Scarbs ain't even that bad.
You make my love seem slanted.
I just can't comprehend it.
Nobody text me while I commune with Osiris,
I needed some shit
with some boom bap in it
and since you picked up,
I know he's not around,
since 3000 Puerto Ricans did
not open their eyes this morning.
You know how that shit go, seagulling
through the 604 with my Bose.
Yo, you deaded me, dog!
I'm on some Marvin Gaye shit.
I don't eat pork, I don't mess with cops.
I took you to the egg place,
then the Park Lane Presidential—
shout out dope piano bar
with the salted snack poles.
Someone said to me, it's like your girlfriend
is our very own Beyoncé,
I ain't g'on lie
I felt proud.
Every so often the place was maximum rain:

red, black and green on my body
'cause I'm dipped in the dreams
of Marcus Garvey,
I go give you every-ting
no matter from my pocket
or my grandfather's wallet.
My winter diet is champagne
and caviar, quick-delivered by Ferrari.
Yo this bee really tryna
come for me eh?! Run up freak!
This Arizona is mad bless right now.
Wagwan my G?!!, motorcycles scream
past the window,
Manchu Wok is lit right now,
you ain't gonna get it all
anymore-real-pathways-to-Socialism
when today unbelievably,
that's the beauty of the streets.
I'm no climate change expert.
I'm a climate change survivor.
God's plan.
Holy Summer Controlla rollin'
deep in a Duppy mind,
even when we knelt, some still felt
threatened, pelted words at us,
but them shits just slid off, meltin'—
if we ever get another chance to
we may "pull-up, pull-up" in the month of May.
You can take that to the masked
banker, police helicopters hoovering

our row houses
the whole summer
while automatic gunfire fetes
the hometown champs.
In its light we do not stunt.
For damned sure, we're turnt up:
a bomb heat cyclone
all up in our feelings.
The feeling that ate the soft zone.
The feeling that lit the clouds,
each muraled block.
In its light we still.
In its stilled light.

I'm Your Migrant Worker, That's What I Am

Design against the elements.
The lightness of the great.
The greatness of the child.
Just kinda what a full-on
kinda O.G. communist *mechanica*
sincera would do. Sincere
and utterly Peruvian cosmo-tectonics:
solar absence, intellectual lit-lit
trolley train. I understand all
of it on two flutes,
as for the others they can jerk me off.
"I'm going through a consuming roses phase."

Bean Pies on a Point Breeze Stoop

What about our
non-disclosure agreement?

Just smoking
big bowls,

eating junk
and writing

like a mother.
Signing and

signing and
signing.

Correct.
Correct.

Who got them sparks
                    looping?
I got them sparks
                    looping.

All them young Negroes still look up at me.

What's the deal with that?
Don't forget the co-sign.

I love driving
around

in my red
drop top.

I aspire
to a trap house.

Poppin' tags,
not microchip flipping. Nah,

like the English
Settlers ripping

and running away
with the Indians' home.

I came here to purchase
I had a ski mask on.

For the whole interview
I had a black ski mask

on my Black face
and it made even

the Black
hip-hop radio hosts

nervous.
My mother said

I been
poppin' tags.

Whatever
that means.

Entire Road in "D"

Riding the tribal sea, doughy boat with its small doors
flying open and closed repeatedly,
letting in the spray like peels of far arrows coming dead at us

frantic and fruitful. In the scarlet muscled hours,
our balcony eye soared amidst the terrible
horse sounds, passing outside high vine-covered walls, a war cadence.

At first, I thought you said you found this beat
as I lugged my brain through the windowsill
into the color L, the last prisoner on that particular floor, inventing
     in a daze

and no one trying to stop me.
I greeted the lost sentence in science
electrically monotonous on my fast tom-tom, as if I were

"I, the human last smother." No one did anything either.
Not the poor grey question, first doubled over the truck
then jumping all turbine mode at the real core horizon.

Not the tens of hundreds owing a sin, which variously plagues me.
Not the various plagues. I too own one major movement door
ridden as a chemical dose.

No wonder they help us forget the here
where everything feels floaty: the deafening
ammo-carrying lorries, tall egg shadows,

tan powder poured over sores whipped into us.
Carrion hardens the sun. It is said that after brawling
we devour the alien, honestly. I see why.

"Not a Violation of the Laws of Nature but a Rare Occurrence."

My minor trickle loosing its way through town,
all roofs red, redder in the stalled December summer,
beckoning as if people, wind-battered bricks were an afterthought,
corrects itself while losing itself on a map-less amble,
yet ever cool are the seawalls and long their sweep
under a hopeful sign just over there, billboard for beer
leering its restless leer among rolling acres of yellow flowers
pointing to the near impossibility of continuity, as mud minarets
bristling with sticks reduce the surrounding huts to general landscape
bedecking any season. Soon a man started shouting
from his boat. His hair matted with thought and the red perfume
of forces on horseback, rifles sheathed in saddles
as one flame-wreathed town burns into another.
Soon a faraway man on a fortress wall, holding
a stick with cloth bag tied to its end poking the large tree
for fruit, while the datum curls ever closer, higher
unfurling away. One story has the man running
through deserts to another man
and so on until the last runs five days unceasing, dying
with news in his throat. Well, sure, a messenger's task is uneasy
but not for the obvious reasons, a wandering shoreline
continually imagined as its previous iteration though the orchard
of miniature berry trees blooms on schedule.
The trees seem to fade more each year. The redness
left on the ground believes itself a perfected plan, and why not,
"To step on it is like stepping on a swarm of flies."

The Rio Communiqué

Gusts thwacked tarps. Meat smells ricocheted
plank to post. We gave up as we can, to another goal;
green fruit. No way to know at that moment
a marauding group with a megaphone

filed toward the *Candomblé* sector, throwing political shadows
like the Mont Ste. Marie snow-making machine noise
twisting narrowly past boulders, ice shelves—
steep banked too savage for anything but

caterpillar treads—the sound's angle tipped up on its sharpest edge
each pine needle felt as winter's advent
but also, the clarity that months and months of silence
had ended battering every feather, signaling the strangest

permanence. No snow in this part of the hemisphere,
we remember how to use the bowl of teeth, the tealeaf headdress.
The specter shuffles closer, farther, waiting, wending like a wasp,
a field of wasps, unfinished, pointing the way.

There's Not Much Hope for Work Here

Not a plateau exactly,
more of the temptation
to test our silo against privation
in the cobblestone alleys
secreting streets while trying
to focus on the utter lack
we're supposed not to notice
jubilating in the communal
activity-postponing hole. That's
where. The basking
in the dead glow
of the experiential skim-boarding
the surplus incredible storings,
displaying an openness to not much,
yet able to detach a series
of objects made from wind
and the locket it's inscribed in,
exiting the flamelight of a nearly
arrived event, flash frozen
in spiced leaves. Perhaps this is why
I nonetheless continue to fear
the geared wheels of disembarkation,
listing and victorious, me from you
and you from our sister,
the cloud-streaked night sky.
But back to your epistolary sonata:
we need a glass eye
and we need a human to share it.

A Few Used Doilies

A moment came when I should have said something,
even so, I would like, in this deserted old village
of colonial churches, drifting sea birds,
to feel part of a larger thinking both historical and mine

prior to the inevitable turning into a revered
monument shaped of a stranger's reverie
since all that gets done is much too concerned
with friendships and partial misunderstandings

of what fits and the disfiguring process happens
with time, anyway and just for this reason
those concerns are least respected, thus passively
left alone to languish amidst the roadside frog calls.

But others might say no to such infinite dreams in a case
recommending instead that we, in these cheerily oblivious
hours, direct ourselves from manners resisting such outward
sensations once the tidal powers recede from our feet.

The man outside the flat sells frozen green fruit juice
in plastic tubes scored with ice etchings, like the stilled
breath of flies. And that's not to think of those
who laughed on the street in the past.

The Nervous Hunger of an Ox

Something has eaten into it while we slept
in our compass, amidst the forest of arms,
and arrayed our phantom refusals,
the sensation of someone watching
you in front of the police station.
The words we chose didn't acquiesce;
the game was called because of darkness.
In this way it feels almost impossible
not to begin cataloguing, during
the blissy weeks of beginning with a guard
car outside, the sort of pressure that
weather responds to
numerically, as with our phobias.
And who knows if more high-minded inshallahs
awaited us besides those shear haircuts
in Smolensk. All we know for sure
is the coming past continues to awaken us
with its undiscovered negations like birdsong
from one of those trains. I hated it too but did
not fight again. I went the other way,
found my place and work
among those who are afraid.

Tuesday

A question hangs in the air like a hoped-for fear,
sunlit steeples balance in the purring snow,
and you frequently feel the same deficit sitting or standing
in line for tickets, a cataract assessment, the river's spray misting
    the balcony.
One thing leads to another torn from the ultimate fighting ring
    tone music.
You can pretend not to eat light
in the *palapa* where such things are done
but the more the day progresses the less things will become.
The far-off bus chugs along, silently. No wet fur smell
escaping through the cinderblock roof hole—
we lie down with the morning removed from our bags of rain.

You Do You

Arm raised in side

salute, mortuary

of a periodic sneeze.

It slays.

It exclaims

its protruding blackness

pressurized by an ice bolt

in the chamber.

Two in the clip,

one in the sunk tit,

protecting a

lean in no meeting

Tuesday cubed multitude

of chanters in so far as

I am beginning

to tell others,

the life he wanted ramen-ing

itself as a wave pool

caught on the emphasis

and Nordic dead gruel

in the quelled

expeller press producing

a whole lotta

hot chicken, Black history.

Notes

During the time I worked on this book, seven poets who were also my teachers passed away.

"Glock Weather" is dedicated to the memory of Philip Levine.

"The Map" is dedicated to the memory of Agha Shahid Ali.

"Tuesday" is dedicated to the memory of Patrick Lane.

"The Rio Communiqué" is dedicated to the memory of Galway Kinnell.

"A Few Used Doilies" is dedicated to the memory of Eavan Boland.

"Modern" is dedicated to the memory of Marie Ponsot.

"The Nervous Hunger of an Ox" is dedicated to the memory of Donald Hall.

Acknowledgments

Thank you to the editors of the following publications in which these pieces first appeared, sometimes in different forms: the *Baffler*; *Berkeley Poetry Review*; *Canada and Beyond*; the *Capilano Review*; the *East Bay Review*; *Eleven Eleven*; the *Ex-Puritan*; *From the Fishouse*; *Hobo Magazine*; *Lana Turner*; *Literary Hub*; the *Malahat Review*; *Obsidian*; *Resistance Journal*; the *Walrus*; and *Washington Square Review*.

"Country Music" was reprinted in the *Printemps des Poètes* Exhibition at the Lazaret Cave, Nice, France (2021); "S.T.A.R.S." was reprinted in *The Best Canadian Poetry* (2018); "Entire Road in 'D'" was reprinted in *Mantis* (2009); and "The Map," was reprinted in *Revival: An Anthology of Black Canadian Writing* (2006).

This work was made possible by support from the American Academy in Rome, the Banff Centre for Arts and Creativity, the Bocas Lit Fest in Trinidad, the Canada Council for the Arts, the Chalmers Arts Fellowship, the K. M. Hunter Charitable Foundation, the Ontario Arts Council, Stanford University, Temple University, the University of Calgary's Distinguished Writers Program, the University of Victoria, the Wallace Stegner Fellowship, and Western Kentucky University.

I am grateful to have been able to write this book while living in a number of places whose geographies shaped the poems: Accra, Barcelona, Bowling Green, Busua, Cabo San Lucas, Calgary, Havana, Honolulu, Iowa City, Itaparica, Lisbon, Madrid, Montreal, Nashville, Norwich, Oakland, Ottawa, Paris, Philadelphia, Port of Spain, Rio de Janeiro, Rome, Salvador, San Francisco, Santa Cruz, Santiago, Sayulita, Stanford, Tobago, Todos Santos, Toronto, Turin, Vancouver, Victoria, and Volterra.

For making this book, I thank Jared Bland, Dionne Brand, Karen Copp, Christie Hanson, Kimberlee Hesas, Kelly Joseph, Mark Levine, Ruta Liormonas, Canisia Lubrin, Jim McCoy, Andrew Roberts, and Sean Tai.

For everything else, I thank Modei Akyea, David Austin, Tim Black, Archie Book, Kimberley Book, Lorna Book, Neilesh Bose, Kwame Dawes, Jennifer Foerster, Forrest Gander, Adrian Harewood, Brenda Hillman, T. Geronimo Johnson, Asad Kiyani, David Lau, Sam Liu, Teresa McWhirter, Karen Ostrom, Eleonora Raspi, Cole Swensen, Valerie Tenning, Yaya, and Alessandro Zangirolami.

Kuhl House Poets

Christopher Bolin
Anthem Speed

Christopher Bolin
Ascension Theory

Christopher Bolin
Form from Form

Shane Book
All Black Everything

Shane Book
Congotronic

Oni Buchanan
Must a Violence

Oni Buchanan
Time Being

Michele Glazer
fretwork

Michele Glazer
*On Tact, & the Made
Up World*

David Micah Greenberg
Planned Solstice

Jeff Griffin
Lost and

Hajar Hussaini
Disbound

John Isles
Ark

John Isles
Inverse Sky

Aaron McCollough
Rank

Randall Potts
Trickster

Bin Ramke
Airs, Waters, Places

Bin Ramke
Matter

Michelle Robinson
The Life of a Hunter

Vanessa Roveto
bodys

Vanessa Roveto
a women

Robyn Schiff
Revolver

Robyn Schiff
Worth

Sarah V. Schweig
Take Nothing with You

Rod Smith
Deed

Donna Stonecipher
Transaction Histories

Cole Swensen
*The Book of a Hundred
Hands*

Cole Swensen
Such Rich Hour

Tony Tost
Complex Sleep

Pimone Triplett
Supply Chain

Nick Twemlow
*Attributed to the Harrow
Painter*

Susan Wheeler
Meme

Emily Wilson
The Keep